To Gordon
Fr

Other books in this series:
HAPPY ANNIVERSARY
To a very special DAD
To a very special DAUGHTER
To a very special FRIEND
To a very special GRANDDAUGHTER
To a very special GRANDMA
To a very special GRANDPA
To a very special GRANDSON
Wishing you HAPPINESS

To my very special HUSBAND
Someone very special…
   TO THE ONE I LOVE
To a very special MOTHER
To a very special SISTER
To a very special SON
To a very special TEACHER
To my very special WIFE

Published in 1998 by Helen Exley Giftbooks in Great Britain.
This revised edition published in 2008

12 11 10 9 8 7 6 5 4 3

ISBN 13: 978-1-84634-290-5

Dedicated to my own special brother, Deon – Helen

Helen Exley Giftbooks, 16 Chalk Hill, Watford, Herts WD19 4BG, UK.
www.helenexleygiftbooks.com

To a very special®
BROTHER

WRITTEN BY PAM BROWN
ILLUSTRATED BY JULIETTE CLARKE
EDITED BY HELEN EXLEY

We share so much – the memories
of our upbringing, our parents,
our early days.
You will always be close,
a very special part of my life.

HELEN EXLEY®

THANK YOU FOR EVERYTHING

Thank you for always being there for me –
however many the miles between us.
Your voice on the phone, remembering
my birthday, your writing on an envelope,
an e-mail with vital news, your special knock,
your grin, the sure clasp of your hand – mean
it is all going to come right.

A good brother looks at a rotten fence post,
a gap in the floorboards, a leaking pipe –
and sighs and says "I'll have a go...."
And does.
Thank you for rescuing me so often.
And all for the price of a cup of tea.

Thank you for persuading me when I left home
that the garage was far enough for one evening.
Thank you for bringing me out a Coke
and a sandwich.
Thank you for getting me back in before
our parents noticed that I'd gone.

Thank you for being there when I've needed you.
For mending things and unravelling things
and backing me up when I felt all alone.
How does any girl manage without a brother?

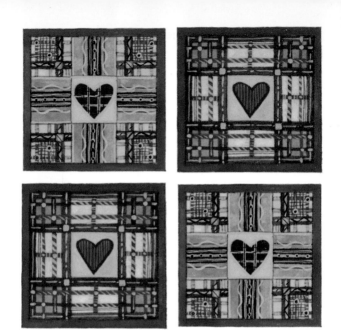

TOTAL SUPPORT

A brother somehow makes you feel secure.

Anchored into life. Certain that whatever happens

someone will be there to help you up,

dust you down and set you on your way.

A contemporary who understands your hopes

and your fears. Always.

The noisiest of brothers can miraculously
become the quietest when you are poorly.

Wherever you go, whatever you do,
somehow your brother is there.

A loving brother is the best comfort in distress.

All brothers and sisters see each other's beginnings.
Know the struggles and mistakes, the excitement.
They shout each other on.
And cheer the victories.
And give each other courage in the darker days.

Brothers warn, scold, growl, complain – but are
always there when you really need them.

A good brother is the anchor that never breaks or
shifts in any storm. Holds fast forever.

KIND AND STRONG

A kind brother can see you through a lifetime.

Brothers can clear drains and paint ceilings
and take cuttings and find out why
your computer is playing up.
You've always been there when I needed you.
You help to hold my life together.
With a tack or two, a length of sellotape,
a bit of string, a dab of glue.
And a kind arm round my shoulders.

Even enormous elder brothers can be
very understanding when it comes to
the funeral of a pet mouse.

Everything brothers do has affection in it.
And so is extra special.

Brothers scold and criticize, but when they praise you, you know you've done wonders. Brothers get cross if you sniffle but know when you are really ill or really unhappy – and help sort things out. Brothers are there when you need them. Kind and funny and strong.

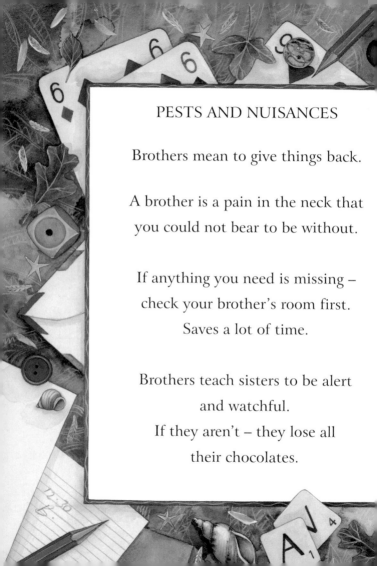

PESTS AND NUISANCES

Brothers mean to give things back.

A brother is a pain in the neck that
you could not bear to be without.

If anything you need is missing –
check your brother's room first.
Saves a lot of time.

Brothers teach sisters to be alert
and watchful.
If they aren't – they lose all
their chocolates.

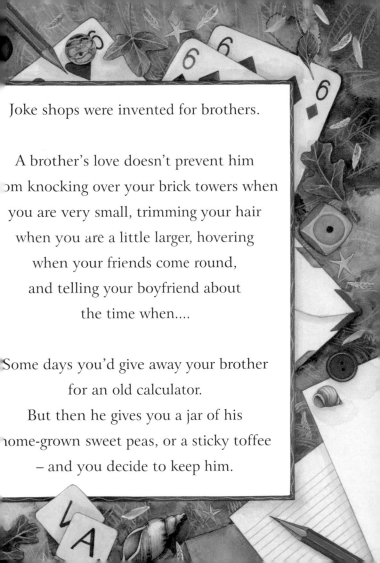

Joke shops were invented for brothers.

A brother's love doesn't prevent him
om knocking over your brick towers when
you are very small, trimming your hair
when you are a little larger, hovering
when your friends come round,
and telling your boyfriend about
the time when....

Some days you'd give away your brother
for an old calculator.
But then he gives you a jar of his
home-grown sweet peas, or a sticky toffee
– and you decide to keep him.

NO ONE KNOWS ME SO WELL

Such a big world and everything to learn.

So many strangers. So many choices.

How good to know you're there –

my companion, my friend.

With you I can relax and smile, knowing you

understand, and accept me as I am.

No one is quite like a brother for no one
knows so much about you.
No one understands the reasons for
everything you do as he does.

We have seen each other
as no one else has ever done.
Scared out of our wits by owls and shadows.
Muddied and bloodied in fights.
Weeping for hidden sorrows.
And so, we're bound close forever.

There isn't any other relationship quite like
that of brothers and sisters – the memories
and the affection will always run deep beneath
all other loves.

However difficult the road ahead
we'll travel it together.

THEY SEE RIGHT THROUGH ME

Conceit doesn't last long in a family.
They read the press notices
– and fall about laughing.

A brother is never put out by changes in your
status or appearance.
He will continue to know that underneath
you are the sister he had to retrieve from
the garage roof!

By now we have grown into respected people.
Fairly dignified.
Reliable. Perhaps a little dull
– but true and tried.
No one suspects that we will always
relish our memories
of mud and scummy ponds
and clambering in trees.

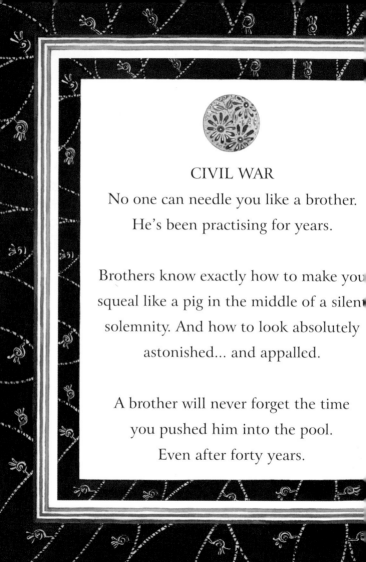

CIVIL WAR

No one can needle you like a brother.
He's been practising for years.

Brothers know exactly how to make you
squeal like a pig in the middle of a silent
solemnity. And how to look absolutely
astonished... and appalled.

A brother will never forget the time
you pushed him into the pool.
Even after forty years.

You always know when you're talking
too much. Your brother is standing
directly behind your friend –
making duck faces.

A day when a brother falls for a
plastic biscuit, a rubber fried egg or
a puddle of imitation ink on their
homework is never a day wasted.

Brothers have a way of saying something
loving or funny or sad
– the very moment you'd decided to
drop them over the local bridge.
That's how abominable brothers survive.

IDIOTS, OAFS AND SILLY-BILLIES

Brothers, from babyhood onwards, have
an affinity with mud.

Turn your back on a brother for a second,
and he's gone. Locked in the bathroom.
Half-way up a ladder.
Stuck in a tree.

Brothers' knees heal slowly – because they keep
lifting up the band-aid to check.

We can put men on the moon – but no one as yet
has found a way to keep up a brother's socks.

Brothers stand on your bed to reach
a shelf – in muddy boots.

Brothers remember one's birthday –
usually about three weeks late.

Brothers are often wonderfully gifted in
making up excuses – the trouble is,
they can get carried away.
Few teachers will accept the fact that a jaguar
barred the way to school – or that
a flash flood disabled the computer.

The games brothers organize are louder,
dirtier and far more dangerous than other games.
More fun.

MEMORIES TO KEEP

A brother holds a thousand memories
of our shared lives – mud-smeared, grass-stained,
jammy-mouthed – drumming our heels in fury,
locked in soundless grief, laughing until we
toppled from our chairs!

I treasure them all – the plots, the secrets,
the surprises. The times you rescued me.
The times I rescued you. And we still do.
There will be greater loves – but none so deeply
rooted as that between siblings.

Time cannot alter us –
only lend us strange disguises.
Others will be fooled – see us
as brave or as cowards,
strong or weak, achievers or failures.
But we will see one another as we have always been.
You are and always will be the brother of
my childhood
– as kind, as constant
– as mischievous, as loving.

To the world we may look capable, efficient –
even sophisticated.
But you and I will remember mud and bonfires,
the solemn burial of our cat, dressing up and
sword fights. Shared secrets. Shared terrors.
Shared laughter.
I raise my glass to us....
The real you. The real me.

I'LL TELL MY BROTHER OF YOU!

How could I have survived
without you there to see off bullies,
clean off stinking muck and mud,
find my missing shoes, unravel equations,
lend me your videos?

Brothers seem to regard their sister
as a necessary evil – till she is in trouble.
When they roar to the rescue,
red-eyed and breathing fire.

Brothers are the people you turn to when
no one else will do.

How very good it is to know that one has
a brother who will Sort Things Out.

Brothers and sisters spend most of
their early life getting each other
in and out of trouble.
This can extend into adulthood, and,
given half a chance, to extreme old age.

"I'll tell my brother of you."
The cry goes back to the cave.
The ultimate deterrent.
Thank you for all the times you rescued me.
Or got thumped, trying.

ROOTS, BONDS

A brother's life is so much a part of
your own life – your roots so intertwined
that each of you affects the other
all your days.

How good it is to know
– when I have to be dignified
and sensible and smart,
that someone
will look across and smile
– knowing exactly who I am
knowing how I feel.
My touchstone. My reminder.
My unbreakable link with reality.

New friends, new loves, must guess what
made you what you are. But we have shared
fears and sorrows, triumphs and excitements
and all those sillinesses that families treasure
and that no one else can ever understand.
We've made a splendid team!

Your life and mine are joined together at
the root. Whatever we become,
however different the paths we take,
the memories of shared adventures,
shared sorrows, shared happiness –
will be with us forever and forever.
Dear Brother, Dear Friend....

ALL LIFE LONG

Friends go. Lovers go.
But brothers stay around.
They will sometimes say
"I told you so"
or call you a silly idiot.
Or just think it and say nothing.
But the friendship will be there.
The loyalty.
The love....

All my life I've known that,
however much you growl at times,
however much you tease,
however much you criticize,
you're still my brother and my
friend. We've shared so much,
good and bad. We need each other.
And I hope we always will.

All life long our thoughts and ways interweave –
and bind us. Whatever distance separates us,
whatever circumstance divides us –
we are family.

A brother's love is not confused by sentiment
and dreams – it is an enduring thing
– steady and unchanged by circumstances.
It lasts life long.
A brother knows us as we are.
Accepts us as we are.
And goes on caring, knowing all our faults
and frailties.

No one can be utterly alone with a brother
– a brother like you.
However far away you are I sense your life,
your smile, your kindness, your concern.